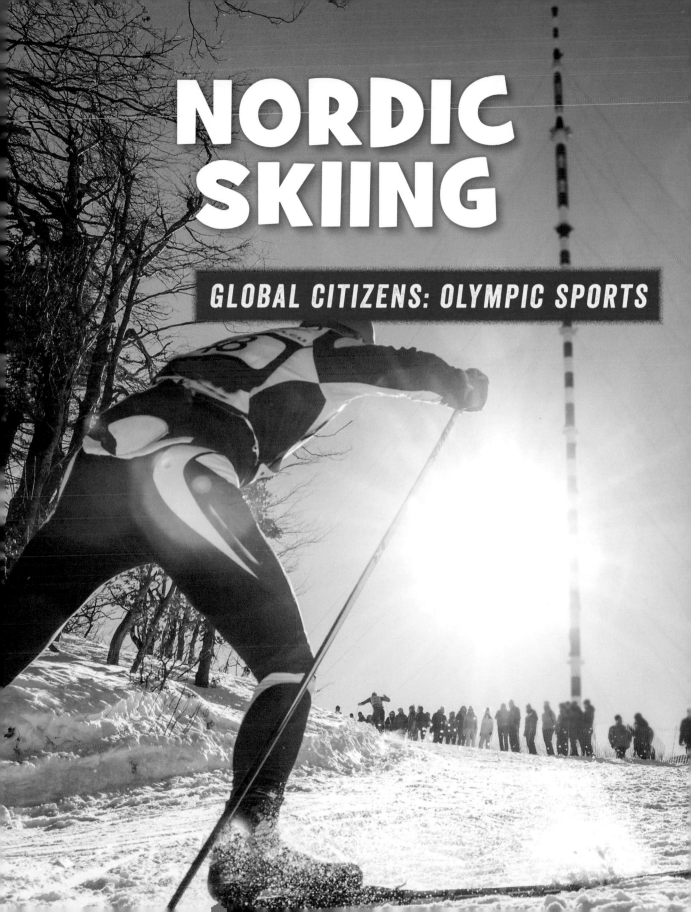

NORDIC SKIING

GLOBAL CITIZENS: OLYMPIC SPORTS

Published in the United States of America by Cherry Lake Publishing
Ann Arbor, Michigan
www.cherrylakepublishing.com

Content Adviser: Liv Williams, Editor, www.iLivExtreme.com
Reading Adviser: Marla Conn MS, Ed., Literacy specialist, Read-Ability, Inc.

Photo Credits: ©kovop58 / Shutterstock.com, cover, 11, 28; ©BNF Gallica / Wikimedia Commons, 5;
Photographed by Suomen Urheilumuseo [1930s] / Wikimedia Commons / Public Domain, 6; ©WikedKentaur /
Wikimedia Commons, 8; ©Guillaume Baviere / flickr.com, 12; ©pleclown / flickr, 13; ©Martynova Anna /
Shutterstock.com, 15, 22, 26; ©Iurii Osadchi / Shutterstock.com, 16; ©StockphotoVideo / Shutterstock.com, 19;
©Petr Toman / Shutterstock.com, 20; ©Piotr Zajac / Shutterstock.com, 21; ©KoreaKHW / Shutterstock.com, 25;
©Weblogiq / Shutterstock.com, 27

Library of Congress Cataloging-in-Publication Data

Names: Labrecque, Ellen, author.
Title: Nordic skiing / Ellen Labrecque.
Description: Ann Arbor, Michigan : Cherry Lake Publishing, 2018. | Series: Global citizens. Olympic sports |
    Includes bibliographical references and index.
Identifiers: LCCN 2017030506 | ISBN 9781534107519 (hardcover) | ISBN 9781534109490 (pdf) |
    ISBN 9781534108509 (pbk.) | ISBN 9781534120488 (hosted ebook)
Subjects: LCSH: Cross-country skiing—Juvenile literature. | Winter Olympics—Juvenile literature.
Classification: LCC GV855.35 .L34 2018 | DDC 796.93/2—dc23
LC record available at https://lccn.loc.gov/2017030506

Cherry Lake Publishing would like to acknowledge the work of The Partnership for 21st Century Learning.
Please visit www.p21.org for more information.

Printed in the United States of America
Corporate Graphics

ABOUT THE AUTHOR

Ellen Labrecque has written over 100 books for children. She loves the Olympics and has
attended both the Winter and Summer Games as a reporter for magazines and television.
She lives in Yardley, Pennsylvania, with her husband, Jeff, and her two young "editors,"
Sam and Juliet. When she isn't writing, she is running, hiking, and reading.

TABLE OF CONTENTS

CHAPTER 1

History: Nordic Skiing

The first Winter Olympics was held in Chamonix, France, from January 25 to February 5, 1924. It included 258 athletes from 16 different countries competing in 16 events. Since then, the Winter Olympics has been held every 4 years in a number of countries. (The Games were skipped in 1940 and 1944 during World War II.) As the Games progressed, more competitors and events were added. Fast-forward to the 2014 Winter Games held in Sochi, Russia. There were 2,873 competitors from 88 different countries competing in 98 events. That's a lot more competitors and events!

From the lightning-speed action in hockey to the graceful acrobatic leaps and turns of figure skating, the Winter Games display some of the most unbelievable sports and athletes. Nordic skiing is no exception—it is one of the hardest, most exhausting events of the Winter Olympics.

A group of Nordic skiers before a relay race in 1937.

The Story of Nordic Skiing

Nordic skiing, most commonly known as cross-country skiing, is when skiers push themselves across flat ground. The sport is the oldest type of skiing. It has been around since 3000 BCE! The sport is named *Nordic* because it was invented in the Nordic region of the world, which includes Finland, Norway, Sweden, Denmark, and Iceland.

In the beginning, people weren't racing on their skis—they were trying to get through deep snow. Nordic skiing officially became a sport in the late 1800s. It was included as a men's sport

Veli Selim Saarinen of Finland won the first Olympic gold medal in cross-country for his country.

in the first Winter Olympics in 1924. The women's teams were added to the Olympic program five Winter Games later, in the 1952 Games in Oslo, Norway. The cross-country events held that first year for men were the 18 kilometer (11.2 miles), 50 kilometer (31 mi), and **Nordic combined**. Thorleif Haug of Norway won all three gold medals. In fact, Norway has won 107 of the total 471 medals awarded in cross-country skiing since the Olympics began!

Skating on Skis

Two different skiing techniques are used in cross-country skiing: classic and freestyle. In classic, the ski boots are only connected to the skis using toe bindings. The skis move back and forth in straight lines. The freestyle technique is a lot faster.

Developing Claims and Using Evidence

Nordic skiers go much faster when they use the freestyle technique instead of the classic. They also use shorter skis and longer poles. Look up some stories online about the two techniques. Try to explain the science behind why shorter skis and longer poles help with speed in skiing.

The mass start event was introduced at the 2002 Games in Salt Lake City, Utah.

In freestyle—also referred to as skate skiing or free skate—the skis are shorter, and the ski boots are locked into position using toe and heel bindings. This allows the skier to move side to side like a skater instead of back and forth. The first time the freestyle technique was allowed at the Winter Games was in 1988 in Calgary, Canada—but only as a **demonstration sport**. It was officially added to the Winter Olympic program as an event at the 1992 Games in Albertville, France. Events now alternate between classic and freestyle technique from Olympics to Olympics.

Events

At the 2018 Winter Olympics in PyeongChang, South Korea, Nordic skiers will compete in several different events. The classic technique will be used for all races except the team sprint and part of the skiathlon event.

Men's 30 km (18.6 mi) Skiathlon	*Athletes use classic skis during the first half of the race (15 km or 9.3 mi), then they switch to freestyle skis for the second half.*
Women's 15 km (9.3 mi) Skiathlon	*Athletes use classic skis during the first half of the race (7.5 km or 4.6 mi), then they switch to freestyle skis for the second half.*
Men's 15 km (9.3 mi) and Women's 10 km (6.2 mi) Individual	*Skiers race against the clock in 30-second intervals, with the best skier going last.*
Men's 50 km (31 mi) and Women's 30 km (18.6 mi) Mass Start	*Skiers start at the same time.*
Men's and Women's Individual Sprint	*Skiers race on a 1 km (0.6 mi) course.*
Men's 4 x 10 km (6.2 mi) and Women's 4 x 5 km (3.1 mi) Relay	*Skiers must "tag" the next skier so they can complete their section of the race. The first two laps are classic technique, and the last two laps are freestyle technique.*

CHAPTER 2

Geography: Go North!

Not surprisingly, the wintry countries far north of the equator that established Nordic skiing dominate the Olympic Nordic events. This is especially true for Norway and Sweden, where Nordic skiing is the national sport. The rivalry between these bordering countries is fierce!

At the 2014 Winter Olympics held in Sochi, Russia, 310 athletes from 54 nations participated in one of the Nordic skiing events. As expected, Norway and Sweden were the top countries

Norway fans cheer on their favorite cross-country athlete.

Nicole Fessel of Germany (second) was also a top athlete at the 2014 Games, winning bronze in the 4 x 5 km (3.1 mi) relay.

Sweden and Norway also dominate the Youth Olympics in the cross-country events.

competing for a spot on the podium. Norway and Sweden tied, with both countries winning 11 medals each. Norway took the lead, however, with five gold medals.

Norway

Norway has won a total of 107 Olympic medals in cross-country skiing, including 40 gold. The country boasts many amazing Nordic skiers, but fans claim Bjorn Daehlie is simply the greatest of all time. His nickname was Rocketman because he skied so fast. At his first Winter Games, he went home with a total of four medals, three of which were gold. In all, he won 12 Olympic medals—eight gold and four silver—for his country in the 1992, 1994, and 1998 Games. The only other athlete who has this many Olympic medals in the sport is Ole Einar Bjoerndalen. He achieved this feat during the 2014 Games in the biathlon, an event that combines cross-country skiing and rifle shooting.

Gathering and Evaluating Sources

Using the Internet or your local library, look at a map of the Nordic region. Name the countries and territories that make up this area. Compare this list to the top ranking countries in Olympic Nordic skiing during the 2014 Games. What countries performed well despite not being part of the Nordic region?

Biathlon made its debut at the 1960 Games in Squaw Valley, California.

Kalla celebrates her win at the 2014 Games.

Sweden

Sweden has won a total of 74 medals, including 29 gold. One of Sweden's best and most popular athletes is Charlotte Kalla. She has won five Olympic medals, including two gold—one at the 2010 Games and another at the 2014 Games. The 2010 win in the individual cross-country event was especially exciting as Sweden had not placed first in the event since the 1968 Games. During the 2014 Games, in the 4 x 5 km (3.1 mi) relay, Kalla took home gold when it looked nearly impossible. Because of her extraordinary win, an airport near her hometown changed its name to Kalla International Airport.

CHAPTER 3

Civics: Olympic Pride

Hosting the Olympic Games can be a big source of pride for the city and the people who live there. It gives the citizens a chance to show off where they live to the entire world. Also, the athletes and fans who come to the Games spend a lot of money there. One of the biggest ways the host country shows off is at the opening and closing ceremonies. More than 3 billion people watched the opening of the 2014 Winter Games.

Russian fans show their support at the 2014 Olympic cross-country ski stadium.

Ingvild F. Ostberg is one of Norway's favorite skiers. She won gold and silver at her 2014 Olympic debut.

The Most Watched

Norwegians love watching their Winter Olympics. They especially love Nordic skiing. More than 4 million people in Norway watched the Olympics on television during the 2014 Games. This number is impressive as the entire country has just 5 million people. The men's cross-country relay was the most popular. More than 1.6 million people watched the event. It was the most watched sports broadcast in Norway since 2011.

Many Norwegians watch the events up close from the sidelines!

Russia might not be allowed to compete at the
2018 Winter Paralympics in PyeongChang.

Cheating to Win?

Russia desperately wanted to win at the 2014 Games, especially since they were the host city. However, they may have cheated to do so. Fourteen of their 20 cross-country skiers were accused of using drugs to make them go faster. Six of these skiers were eventually suspended from competing. As of 2017, it was still being determined whether these banned skiers would be allowed to compete at the 2018 Winter Olympics and **Paralympics** in PyeongChang, South Korea.

Developing Claims

*Russia isn't the only country whose athletes were accused of using drugs to **enhance** their skills during the Winter Olympics. Since the 1972 Winter Games, athletes from 14 other countries have been caught using drugs. Almost all of the athletes who placed were stripped of their medals. Use the Internet and your local library to research more about athletes who cheated in the Winter Olympics. Why might an athlete choose to cheat? Using the evidence you found, develop an opinion on the matter.*

Economics: Nordic Skiing Is Big Business

Hosting the Olympic Games costs a lot of money! PyeongChang has spent $1.5 billion on the ski resort for the 2018 Games! This doesn't include the cost of any of the other **venues**—even the stadium for the opening and closing ceremonies. The city hopes to earn back a lot of that money once the Olympics begins.

The Fans

Tourists spend money by staying in hotels, buying souvenirs, and eating in the city's restaurants. Americans aren't big fans of Nordic skiing, but countries like Sweden and Norway are. It is the most popular Winter Olympic sport in Norway. Many Nordic

The Alpensia Cross-Country Centre in PyeongChang, South Korea, will hold approximately 7,500 people!

Fans watch their favorite athletes race to the finish line.

fans will fly in to see the events. Others will watch the events unfold on television or stream them online. Discovery Communications paid $1.45 billion to broadcast the Olympics in 2018 and through to 2024. During the 2014 Winter Olympics, close to 1.6 million of Norway's 5 million citizens watched the biggest Nordic skiing races. This is a third of the entire country!

Biathlon is one of Europe's favorite Olympic sports to watch.

Spyder has been the US Ski Team's official clothing sponsor since 1989.

Taking Informed Action

Do you want to learn more about the Winter Olympics and Nordic skiing? There are many different organizations that you can explore. Check them out online. Here are three to start your search:

- USSA—Nordic: Learn more about the US Nordic Ski Team on its official website.
- Olympic—Cross-Country Skiing: Discover more about the history of Nordic skiing at the Olympics.
- International Skiing History Association—Cross-Country Skiing: Read more about how Nordic skiing became an official sport.

[21ST CENTURY SKILLS LIBRARY]

The Sponsors

Advertisers like Coca-Cola and McDonald's pay a lot of money to sponsor the Olympics. Their signs and logos appear on television in commercials and on boards all over the venues. Clothing companies supply the athletes' uniforms and their outfits for the opening and closing ceremonies. The US Olympic skiing team also has its own sponsors, such as the outdoor clothing companies L.L. Bean and Spyder. Skiers have to wear the Olympic uniform, but they can use equipment and other gear made by other companies. Nordic skiers use wax on their skis to help them go faster. Fast Wax sponsors skiers to use their brand during the Games. Although fans can't see the actual wax, the skiers can talk about using the wax in commercials and in advertisements.

Communicating Conclusions

Before reading this book, did you know much about Nordic skiing and the Winter Olympics? Now that you know more, why do you think the sport isn't as popular in the United States as it is in other countries? Share what you learned about the sport with friends at school or with your family at home.

Think About It

In many Olympic sports, it takes far longer for women to participate in the Games. In Nordic skiing, women weren't given the opportunity to compete for Olympic glory until 28 years after the first time men were. Why do you think the Nordic women's events weren't included at the same time as the men's? Research this topic further using the Internet and your local library. Use the data you find to support your answer.

For More Information

Further Reading

Burns, Kylie. *Biathlon, Cross-Country, Ski Jumping, and Nordic Combined.* New York: Crabtree Publishing, 2010.

Vordenberg, Pete. *Momentum: Chasing the Olympic Dream.* Williamston, MI: Out Your Backdoor Press, 2002.

Wallechinsky, David, and Jaime Loucky. *The Complete Book of the Winter Olympics.* Hertford, NC: Crossroad Press, 2014.

Websites

The International Olympic Committee
https://www.olympic.org/the-ioc
Discover how the IOC works to build a better world through sports.

International Ski Federation—Cross Country World Cup
www.fis-ski.com/cross-country
Learn more about Nordic skiing competitions all over the world.

GLOSSARY

demonstration sport (dem-uhn-STRAY-shuhn SPORT) a sport that is played in order to promote it

enhance (en-HANS) to make something bigger or better

Nordic combined (NOR-dik kuhm-BINED) Olympic sport in which athletes compete in both the cross-country skiing and ski jumping events

Paralympics (par-uh-LIM-piks) an international competition, like the Olympics, but for physically disabled athletes

tourists (TOOR-ists) people who are traveling for pleasure

venues (VEN-yooz) places where actions or events occur

INDEX